Space Raiders

Simon Cheshire

Editorial consultants:
Cliff Moon and Lorraine Petersen

RISING ★ STARS

nasen
Helping Everyone Achieve

nasen
NASEN House, 4/5 Amber Business Village, Amber Close,
Amington, Tamworth, Staffordshire B77 4RP

Rising Stars UK Ltd.
22 Grafton Street, London W1S 4EX
www.risingstars-uk.com

Text, design and layout © Rising Stars UK Ltd.
The right of Simon Cheshire to be identified as the author of this work has been asserted by him in accordance with the Copyright, Design and Patents Act 1988.

Published 2007
Reprinted 2007

Cover design: Button plc
Illustrator: Enzo Troiano
Text design and typesetting: Andy Wilson
Publisher: Gill Budgell
Commissioning editor: Catherine Baker
Publishing manager: Lesley Densham
Editor: Clare Robertson
Editorial consultants: Cliff Moon and Lorraine Petersen

All rights reserved. No part of this publication may be reproduced, stored in a retrieval system, or transmitted in any form by any means, electronic, mechanical, photocopying, recording or otherwise without the prior permission of Rising Stars UK Ltd.

British Library Cataloguing in Publication Data.
A CIP record for this book is available from the British Library

ISBN: 978-1-84680-203-4

Printed by Craft Print International Limited, Singapore

Contents

Characters — 5

Scene 1: **Mutiny!** — 7

Scene 2: **Attack!** — 17

Scene 3: **Disaster!** — 29

Scene 4: **Battle!** — 37

Drama ideas — 47

Characters

Captain Krell Captain of the raiding spaceship Moonblade.

Sila Lizzik The Moonblade's second-in-command.

Ed Failsafe The pilot of the Moonblade.

Grisk Jackson In charge of the weapons on the Moonblade.

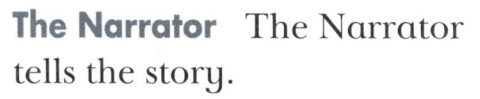

Jonas Finch The Moonblade's cook and handyman.

The Narrator The Narrator tells the story.

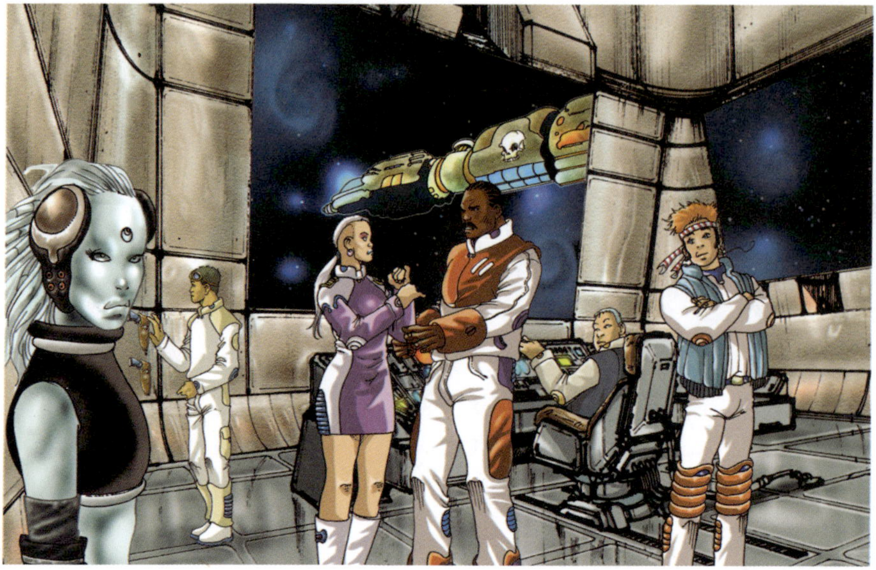

Scene 1
Mutiny!

Narrator It is the year 2179. Humans live on many of the outer planets. This part of space is full of danger.

Captain Krell Faster, Ed! Faster!

Ed Failsafe We're at top speed, Sir!

Grisk Jackson I can't aim the lasers from here! We have to get closer to that ship!

Sila Lizzik Move this bucket of rust, Ed!

Ed Failsafe I can't! We'll break up in space!

Captain Krell   Stand down! All crew stand down. We'll never catch one of those new Tornado ships.

Sila Lizzik   What? You're giving up? You coward!

Captain Krell   Watch your mouth, Sila Lizzik! I give the orders on this ship.

Narrator   This is the space raider Moonblade. Captain Krell is in charge. The Moonblade raids other spaceships and steals from them.

Jonas Finch   I'll just check that the engines are okay, Sir.

Sila Lizzik   Then get us our food, Jonas! And make sure it's better than last time.

Scene 1   Mutiny!

Narrator   Times are hard for the crew of the Moonblade. They have not raided a spaceship for a long time. The crew are hungry and tired.

Jonas Finch   Here's your food. This will have to last you till tomorrow.

Ed Failsafe   Is this it? One tube of dry space food?

Grisk Jackson   Ha! I thought it was boot polish!

Ed Failsafe   I need some proper food.

Grisk Jackson   Let's try some of that. Eurgh! Cleaning boots is all it's good for.

Sila Lizzik   No proper space raider would eat this muck.

Space Raiders

Grisk Jackson Yeah!

Ed Failsafe When was the last time
we had a proper meal?
Spaceburgers and chips …

Grisk Jackson Shut up, Ed –
you're making me hungry!

Jonas Finch I'm sorry, everyone.
That's all we have left.

Sila Lizzik I've killed men for less food
than this! Are we space raiders,
or are we mice?

Grisk Jackson We're space raiders –
or we used to be.

Ed Failsafe Yeah – but it's months since
we've raided anything.

Sila Lizzik Things have got to change
around here – or there'll
be trouble.

Scene 1   Mutiny!

Captain Krell   Lads, lads! I know times are bad. But this is the Moonblade, one of the best raider ships in the galaxy.

Sila Lizzik   Not for much longer, if we go on like this.

Ed Failsafe   I'll starve if I don't get some proper food. I knew I should never have become a raider.

Grisk Jackson   Aww, shut up, Ed.

Captain Krell   Times are hard, lads, but they'll get better. Just work. Work, work and more work, that's what we need now.

Narrator	Captain Krell has been raiding for years. He's seen hard times before, and he has also seen good times. But some of his crew are getting fed up. Later that evening, Sila Lizzik calls the others.

Sila Lizzik	Ed, Grisk, Jonas! Gather round. Where's the captain?
Jonas Finch	Asleep in his bunk. Shall I get him?
Sila Lizzik	No. It's you three I want to talk to.
Grisk Jackson	I'm too hungry to talk.
Ed Failsafe	Yeah – I'm starving.
Sila Lizzik	Stop flapping your lips and listen!

Scene 1   Mutiny!

Narrator	Sila Lizzik is as evil as any raider in the galaxy. She has murdered her way to the top, and she isn't going to stop now.
Sila Lizzik	We have to get rid of Krell. He's holding us back. Without him, we could really go places.
Jonas Finch	You're saying we should mutiny?
Sila Lizzik	The sooner the better.
Jonas Finch	But he's our captain. He saved my life when that cargo ship blew up.
Sila Lizzik	But he's past it. He's lost his nerve.
Ed Failsafe	Well, I'm with Sila. We need food. If that means getting rid of Krell – that's okay with me.

Grisk Jackson I say we should mutiny too.
We could have raided that
Tornado ship, if the captain had
had the guts! My guns never miss!

Sila Lizzik Well, Jonas Finch?
Are you with us, or will I
have to kill you?

Jonas Finch I'm with you, Sila.

Sila Lizzik You'd better be.
I'll be watching you –
all of you.
Got it?

Ed Failsafe Yes, Sila! Of course!

Grisk Jackson Er … yeah!

Jonas Finch Okay, Sila.

Scene 1 Mutiny!

Narrator But Jonas feels bad.
He doesn't want to mutiny
against Captain Krell.

Jonas Finch What can I do?
I can't let Krell down,
but Sila will murder me
if I don't join in the mutiny.
What can I do?

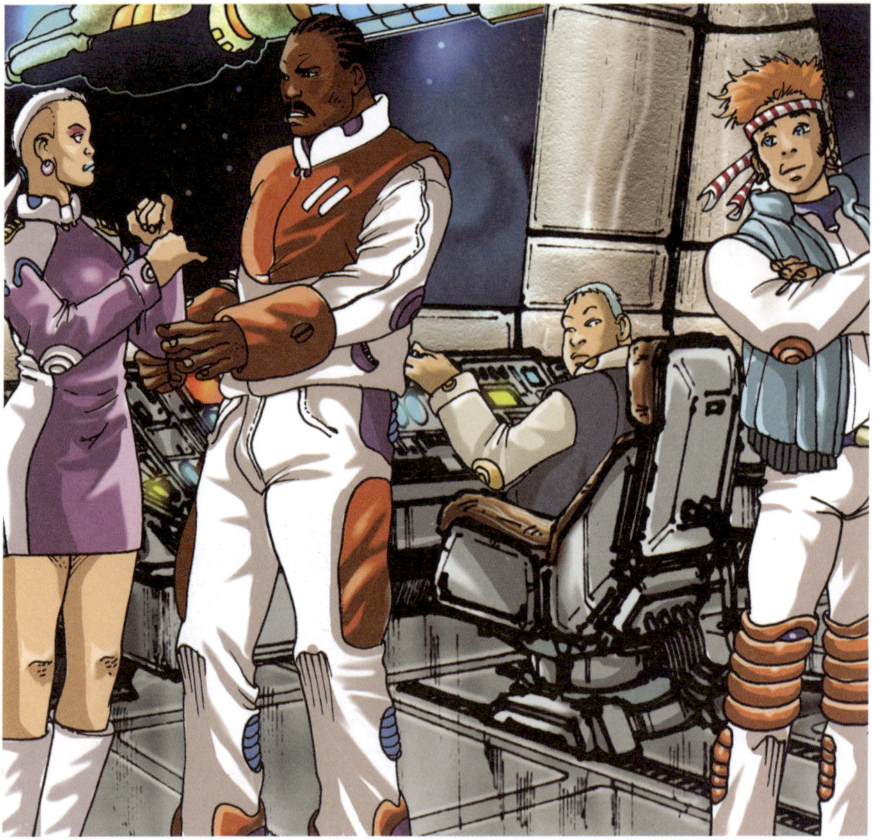

Scene 2
Attack!

Narrator	The next day, all seems to be quiet on board the Moonblade.

Sila Lizzik Are you men ready?

Grisk Jackson I'm ready.

Ed Failsafe I'm ready too.
Or as ready as I can be,
without any food inside me.

Grisk Jackson I used the last of
my food powder
to get a nice shine
on my laser guns.

Ed Failsafe You and your guns!

Grisk Jackson	You'll be glad of my guns when it comes to the battle.
Sila Lizzik	Quiet! Stay low. We don't take over the ship until I say. Okay?
Ed Failsafe	Okay.
Grisk Jackson	Okay.
Sila Lizzik	Where's that worm Jonas Finch? He'd better be ready too, or I'll slice him into pieces.
Narrator	Jonas is with Captain Krell. He is telling him about Sila's plan to mutiny.
Jonas Finch	I've told them that I'm in on the plot, Sir. They think I'll back them up.
Captain Krell	That's smart, boy. Very smart.

Scene 2 Attack!

Jonas Finch   Thank you, Sir.

Captain Krell   But why are you telling me all this? Space raiding is tough. You might get more by being on Sila's side.

Jonas Finch   I won't let you down just because times are hard, Sir. You saved my life once, and now I'll do my best to save yours.

Captain Krell   Quiet, boy! They're here!

Sila Lizzik	Good day to you, Captain!
Captain Krell	So, what's wrong, Lizzik?
Sila Lizzik	Wrong, sir? Why, nothing! What makes you think something is wrong?
Captain Krell	You've never wished anyone good morning in your life. Out with it! What's on your mind?
Grisk Jackson	Shall I get the laser guns, Sila?
Ed Failsafe	Hang on – if you're getting the laser guns, I'm getting my ear plugs!
Sila Lizzik	Shut your mouths, the pair of you! Or I'll shut them for you!
Ed Failsafe	Sorry, Sila.
Sila Lizzik	You will be, Ed. You will be.

Scene 2 Attack!

Narrator Suddenly, there is a loud bang. The whole ship twists in space.

Captain Krell Battle stations! All crew to battle stations!

Sila Lizzik Looks like there's another spaceship coming our way.

Ed Failsafe Oh no!

Grisk Jackson At last! A chance to do some proper raiding!

Jonas Finch We're hit!

Narrator	The crew rush to the controls of the spaceship. There is a second loud bang.

Captain Krell All crew report!

Sila Lizzik Two of the engines are failing!

Grisk Jackson Weapons are down!
I'm trying to get them back online!

Ed Failsafe I'm too scared to look at the read-outs!

Captain Krell Pull it together, Ed!
Fire up the other engines!
Now!

Jonas Finch A very big ship must be firing on us.

Captain Krell Put that ship on screen!
I want to see what pond-sucking scum dares to attack Captain Krell of the Moonblade!

Scene 2 Attack!

Narrator When the ship's scanner is turned on, the crew freeze.
They stare with horror
at what is out there,
right beside them in space.

Grisk Jackson Wow! Look at the guns on that!

Ed Failsafe I can't look!

Captain Krell It's incredible!

Jonas Finch Look at those markings.
That's a Martian drone ship.

Sila Lizzik No, it can't be them!
It can't be them!

Grisk Jackson But – I thought those Martian ships were just a space myth!

Captain Krell That's no myth.
That's the Dead Planet.

Ed Failsafe What's the Dead Planet?

Space Raiders

Space Raiders

Jonas Finch It's the most evil raiding ship
in the whole of space.
You see that extra bit
built on to the side
of the ship?
They had to add
that bit on, to hold
all their loot.

Grisk Jackson They've got stuff that
makes my laser guns
look like paper darts!

Sila Lizzik We're finished!

Ed Failsafe I don't like this!
I want to go home!

Sila Lizzik It's too late for that now,
you cowardly worm!

Ed Failsafe Let me out of here!

Jonas Finch Nobody panic!
There must be something
we can do!

Scene 2 Attack!

Captain Krell It's too late for that, boy. Captain Tholl of the Dead Planet takes no prisoners.

Narrator The crew of the Moonblade seem to be doomed.

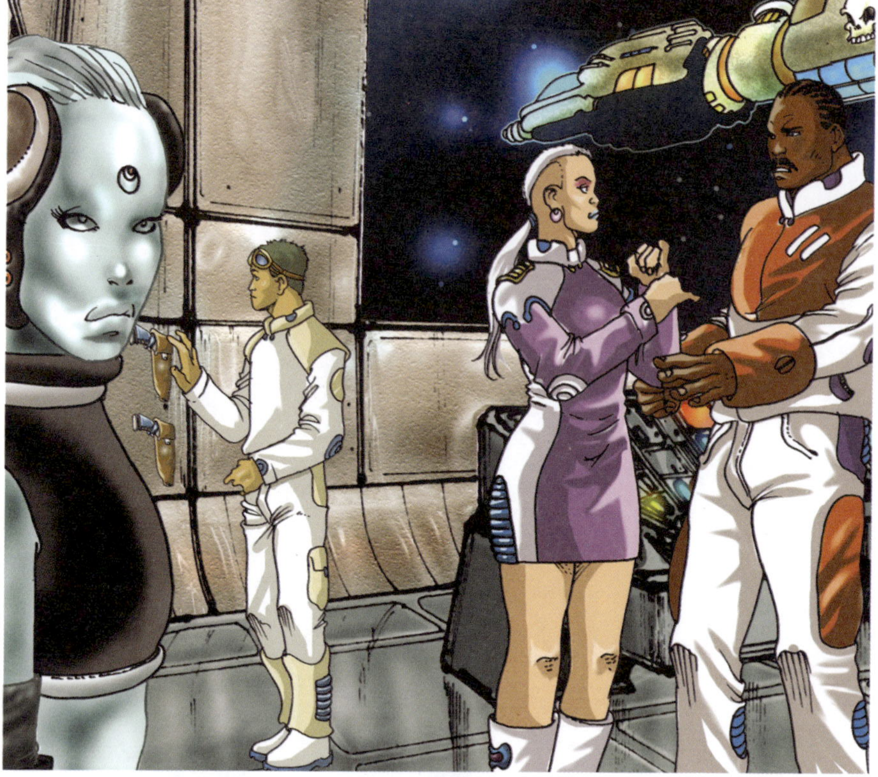

Scene 3
Disaster!

Narrator	The crew of the Moonblade are more scared than they have ever been before. Especially Ed Failsafe.

Ed Failsafe I should have listened to my mother!

Grisk Jackson Why? What did she tell you?

Ed Failsafe I don't know, do I? I didn't listen!

Sila Lizzik Right! I'm taking command! This is a mutiny, Captain Krell!

Captain Krell You low-down worm, Lizzik!

Jonas Finch All of you!
This is no time to argue!
We have to work together!

Grisk Jackson Enough talk!
I say we need action.

Ed Failsafe I say we need to hide!

Sila Lizzik The men are on my side,
Captain. Grisk is right,
we need to take action, fast.

Grisk Jackson We need to fight those
Martians.

Captain Krell You want to *fight* them?

Sila Lizzik Yeah – do you have a problem
with that?

Captain Krell Captain Tholl's gang of thugs
are the toughest band of
raiders in the galaxy.
There are five of us! Five!

Scene 3   Disaster!

Narrator   Another burst of laser fire hits the ship.

Sila Lizzik   We have to get away – now.
If they hit our engines again, we've had it.

Jonas Finch   Yeah – without the engines, we're dead in space.

Ed Failsafe   Thanks for letting us know.

Jonas Finch   Think! There must be something we can do!

Captain Krell   Jonas is right.

Sila Lizzik   Silence!
You've led us into disaster, Krell.
I'm in charge now.
Grisk, man the laser guns!
Ed, get out from under that chair!

Jonas Finch   We can't fight them!

Space Raiders

Grisk Jackson Oh yeah?

Sila Lizzik Prepare for battle!
We fight to the last!

Narrator Grisk Jackson hands out laser guns. Sila Lizzik locks all the ship's doors. Ed Failsafe wishes he was somewhere else.

Sila Lizzik We've got to give it our best shot. We've only got one chance against these Martians. Are you with me, men?

Grisk Jackson Yes!

Ed Failsafe Er – okay.

Captain Krell Maybe Lizzik is right. I've failed you all.

Scene 3 Disaster!

Jonas Finch No, Captain.
We can't beat the crew of
the Dead Planet in a fight.
The only way out of this
is to be smarter than them.

Ed Failsafe Ha! No chance of that!

Grisk Jackson Yeah. We've just got to
blast them.

Sila Lizzik Stand your ground, men!
When they come on board,
shoot to kill!

Grisk Jackson We're ready, Captain Lizzik.

Sila Lizzik Ha! I like the sound of that.
Captain Lizzik.

Narrator The crew wait, holding their
guns tightly in their hands.
They hear a loud clang.

Ed Failsafe That's the airlock!

Jonas Finch	Once they're through that, they'll be all over the ship.
Ed Failsafe	Oh, great!
Sila Lizzik	Shut up, Ed. Just use your head.
Grisk Jackson	And your gun.
Narrator	For a long time, there is no sound. The crew of the Moonblade feel their hearts thump in their chests.
Captain Krell	All my years of raiding. This is how it ends.
Narrator	From deep inside the ship comes the sound of heavy footsteps.
Ed Failsafe	They're here!

Scene 3 Disaster!

Narrator The crew of the Dead Planet are coming – running, shouting, coming to get them!

Grisk Jackson They say the Dead Planet never leaves a trace behind. It'll be like we were never here.

Narrator The Moonblade crew switch on their laser guns and get ready to die.

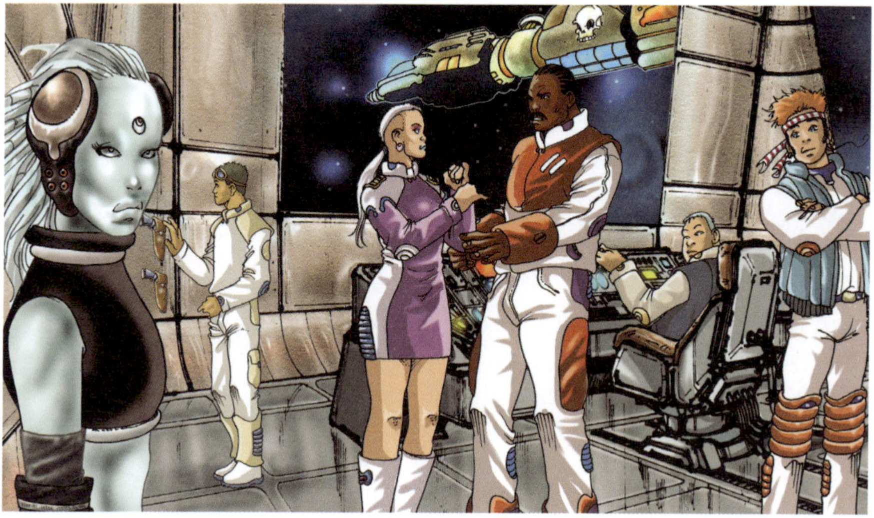

Scene 4
Battle!

Narrator	The crew of the Dead Planet storm the Moonblade.
Sila Lizzik	Are all the inner doors sealed?
Ed Failsafe	Yes.
Sila Lizzik	Keep it that way. Those doors are half a metre thick. They'll slow these gutter rats down.
Narrator	At last, Jonas Finch sees a way out of the trap.
Jonas Finch	Captain Krell, I have an idea.

Captain Krell Don't you ever give up, boy?

Jonas Finch Of course not!
Listen, Captain Tholl and his men have opened the airlock, right?

Captain Krell Yes.

Jonas Finch And what do we use the airlock for?

Captain Krell Why, keeping the air in the ship, of course. I don't…

Narrator But suddenly, Captain Krell can see what Jonas means. There may be hope after all.

Captain Krell Open all the doors, Ed!

Sila Lizzik What? Are you mad? Don't listen to the old fool, Ed! I'm captain now!

Grisk Jackson Yeah – Krell's lost it!

Scene 4 Battle!

Jonas Finch No! Listen to the captain. The *real* captain!

Captain Krell I order you to open the airlock doors! All at once! Do it!

Ed Failsafe But with all the doors open, Tholl's crew will get in! Even worse, we'll all be pulled out into space! The air will rush out!

Jonas Finch Exactly!

Grisk Jackson Now Finch has lost it too!

Narrator Sila Lizzik points her gun at Captain Krell. Her eyes are full of fear.

Sila Lizzik You stay quiet, Krell! Or I'll blast you to Saturn! Crew, get ready to defend the control room! Get ready to fight the Dead Planet!

Ed Failsafe What do I do? What do I do?

Jonas Finch Listen to the captain, Ed. We'll never fight the Dead Planet off! Our only hope is to spit them out into space!

Narrator From the other side of the door come frightening sounds. The sound of weapons being switched on. The sound of the Dead Planet's crew laughing at how easy this raid is.

Scene 4 Battle!

Sila Lizzik You still think we should open the doors? I say we should fight! We live by the laser, we die by the laser!

Grisk Jackson Yeah!

Captain Krell Everyone hang onto something!

Jonas Finch When the airlock doors open, we'll be pulled into space too, unless we're holding on tight!

Narrator Captain Krell aims his laser gun
at the door controls and fires.
The doors begin to move.

Sila Lizzik You madman!
You've killed us all!

Narrator With a screaming howl,
all the air in the ship
shoots out of the airlock.

Captain Krell Hang on! Hold tight!

Narrator The crew of the Moonblade
hold on to chairs and control
panels as tightly as they can.
The crew of the Dead Planet
are ripped away, out of the airlock,
out into space.

Ed Failsafe Look on the scanner!
They're all adrift!
Every last one of them!

Scene 4   Battle!

Captain Krell   Shut the doors! Close the airlock! Pump air back into the ship!

Grisk Jackson   Yes, Captain!

Ed Failsafe   Shutting the doors right away, Captain!

Narrator   Minutes later, everything is quiet again.
The crew are tired, but safe.

Sila Lizzik   I don't believe it.
Nobody can beat Captain Tholl of the Dead Planet.

Grisk Jackson   Well, *we* did.

Jonas Finch   Thanks to the captain.

Ed Failsafe   Piece of cake, really.

Grisk Jackson   Yeah – just look at them all, drifting in space!

Space Raiders

Jonas Finch   That's Captain Tholl's last raid, I reckon.

Sila Lizzik   Well – you were right, Krell. I suppose you'll send me out of the airlock next.

Captain Krell   No, Sila. Anyone can make a mistake. I'm going to pick someone else to be my second-in-command. But you can stay on the crew.

Sila Lizzik   Okay.

Narrator   The crew set to work to mend the ship.

Captain Krell   I must thank you, Jonas. Your plan saved us all. How about being my new second-in-command?

Jonas Finch   I'd be pleased to, Sir.

Scene 4   Battle!

Captain Krell   And I will be a better captain from now on. No more hard times. Now – let's find a nice food transporter ship to raid!

All the crew   Aye aye, Captain!

Drama ideas

After Scene 1

- Hotseating: choose one person to be Jonas Finch.
- Everyone else can ask Jonas questions to find out what he thinks about Captain Krell and Sila Lizzik, and why he can't decide what to do next.
- As a group, decide what you think Jonas should do next and why.

After Scene 2

- With a partner, be Jonas Finch and Ed Failsafe.
- Jonas wants to think of a plan to defeat the Dead Planet – but Ed just wants to panic. Act out their conversation.

Drama ideas

3 After Scene 3

- In your group, decide what you think will happen next. Will the crew of the Moonblade decide to fight the crew of the Dead Planet? Will they win?
- Act out your ideas.

After Scene 4

- With a partner, be Sila Lizzik and Captain Krell.
- They are on another adventure, after the end of the play. Captain Krell needs Sila's help to fight off an enemy. Will Sila help him – or will she let him be defeated?

SuperScripts

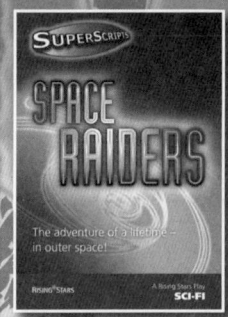

Alien Attack — Tom and Jonno get captured by evil aliens — will they ever escape? *SCI-FI*	**Space Raiders** — The adventure of a lifetime — in outer space! *SCI-FI*	**Champions** — There can only be one winner. *SPORT*	**Truth or Dare?** — Thrills and spills in the high-energy world of skateboarding. *SPORT*
Time Warriors — A dangerous journey to the future. *FANTASY*	**Island Footprints** — Shipwrecked on a desert island ... but who else is there? *FANTASY*	**Payback** — A bully gets taught a lesson he won't forget ... *REAL LIFE*	**King Kevin** — What happens at school when gangs get out of hand? *REAL LIFE*

RISING ★ STARS

PHONE
0870 40 20 40 8

www.risingstars-uk.com